Kids Need to Be Safe

"Julie Nelson demonstrates remarkable sensitivity to the needs and feelings of young children in foster care. I'm confident that countless young children will draw strength and comfort from the clear and simple words Ms. Nelson has written for them. And foster parents and other caregivers will find a wealth of wisdom in the information provided for them, particularly in the 'healing words' to use when children are feeling confused and afraid."

—Martha Farrell Erickson, Ph.D., senior fellow & co-chair
President's Initiative on Children, Youth & Families
University of Minnesota

Kids Need to Be Safe

A Book for Children in Foster Care

BY JULIE NELSON

ILLUSTRATED BY MARY GALLAGHER

**★Kids Are
Important** Series
Help for Troubled Times

free spirit
PUBLISHING®

Text copyright © 2006 by Julie Nelson
Illustrations copyright © 2006 by Mary Gallagher
An edition of this book was first published in 2003 by Lifetrack Resources as *Kids Are Important*.

Library of Congress Cataloging-in-Publication Data
Nelson, Julie.
    Kids need to be safe : a book for young children in foster care / by Julie Nelson ; illustrated by Mary Gallagher.
    p. cm.—(Kids are important)
    ISBN 1-57542-192-5
1. Foster children—United States—Juvenile literature. I. Title. II. Series.
    HV881.N45 2005
    362.73'3'0973—dc22
                                                                                            2005015075

ISBN: 978-1-57542-192-6

Reading Level Grade 1; Interest Level Ages 4–10;
Fountas & Pinnell Guided Reading Level H

Edited by Eric Braun
Cover and interior design by Marieka Heinlen

15 14 13 12 11 10 9 8
Printed in Hong Kong
P17200518

Free Spirit Publishing Inc.
6325 Sandburg Road, Suite 100
Minneapolis, MN 55427-3674
(612) 338-2068
help4kids@freespirit.com
www.freespirit.com

Free Spirit offers competitive pricing.
Contact edsales@freespirit.com for pricing information on multiple quantity purchases.

Dedication

This book is dedicated to children in foster care
and the adults who support them.

Acknowledgments

Thank you to the caring staff of Families Together for supporting the stressed young children in our preschool each day. Thanks also to Lifetrack Resources for its assistance with this project.

Kids are important.
Kids need to be safe.
They need safe places to live,
and safe places to play.

Usually moms and dads take
good care of kids and keep kids safe.

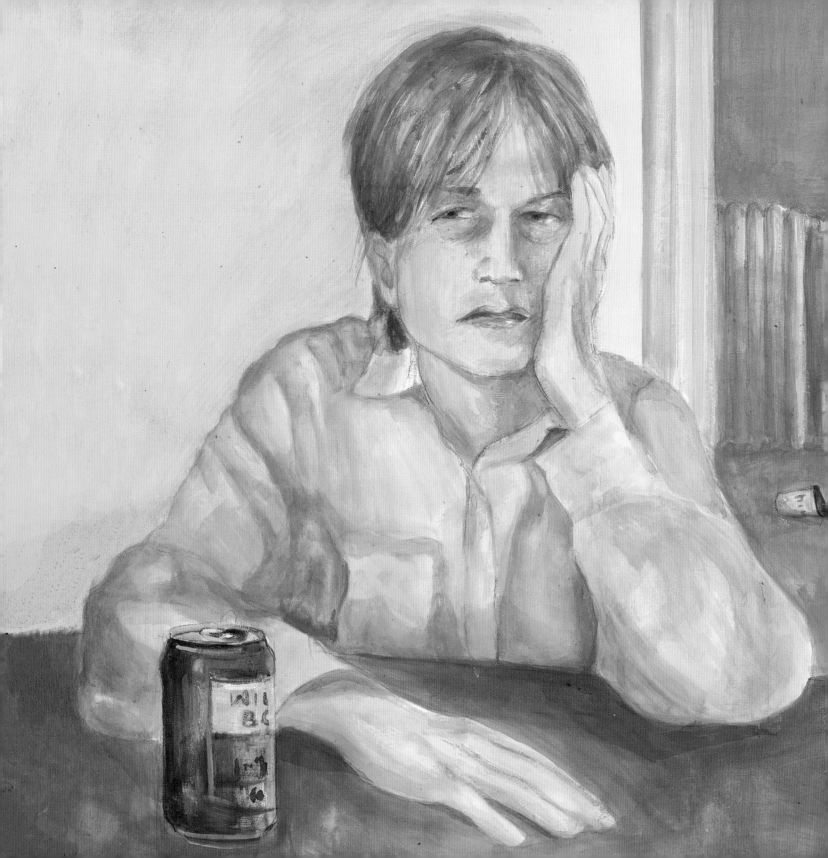

Sometimes it's hard for parents
to take care of kids and keep them safe.
Kids are important.
Kids need to be safe.

Sometimes moms and dads
need to solve big problems—
like finding a place to live,
learning not to drink too much,
or learning not to hurt people
when they are angry.

Sometimes parents need help
taking care of their children.
Grandmas and grandpas might help.
Aunts and uncles might help.

When families have big problems to solve,
other people can help take care of children too.
The police might help.
Social workers and foster parents help too.
Kids are important.
Kids need to be safe.

Foster parents take care of children
when parents need help.
Foster parents have a bed
and food and toys for children.
Foster parents keep kids safe.
Kids are important.
Kids need to be safe.

When kids stay in foster homes
they have many feelings.

They might feel happy,
or sad,
or scared,
or mad,
or lonely.

Parents love their kids
even when they need help
taking care of them.
Kids are important.
Kids need to be safe.

Foster parents take care of kids
because kids are important.
Kids need to be safe.

Providing Support and Encouragement to Stressed Young Children

A message to foster parents, social workers, teachers, and caregivers

Foster placement provides increased safety for the thousands of young children in out-of-home placement, but it also brings loss and fear. Adults who teach and support young children in foster care can provide support and encouragement. You can send messages of hope on the following topics.

SAFETY

Children who have been abused or witnessed family violence may not know if they are safe and may be confused about what is safe. Building trust with a hurting child will take time. Fearful children may appear withdrawn or angry and may interpret limit-setting as being disliked or rejected. Healing words include: *This is a safe place for children. I will keep you safe, me safe, and all the children here safe.*

ACCEPTANCE

Stressed children may feel angry, frightened, worried, sad, or confused. Some children will act out, while others will withdraw. Children need to be accepted and cared for no matter what they are feeling. Help children to understand their feelings and to express emotions in safe ways. Accept emotions while providing limits for inappropriate behavior. Healing words include: *I will take care of you when you are happy, and I will take care of you when you are angry, too. I will take care of you with all your feelings.*

RELAXATION

The stress children experience with a major life change, such as out-of-home placement, is physical as well as emotional. Elevated stress hormones can make it hard for children to sit still. Stressed children may be edgy and quick to act out, with seemingly small problems causing big reactions. Healing activities to do with children include playing in water, playing with clay, dough, or sand, and doing vigorous outdoor exercise. Experiences of non-threatening, nurturing touch can also be healing. Rub lotion on children's hands, paint their fingernails, or push them on a swing. These actions may help stressed children feel more calm.

CONFUSION

The changes that come with out-of-home placement may leave children feeling confused. "What happened?" and "Is it my fault?" are important questions to answer for children. If kids let you know they feel at fault, healing words may include: *Sometimes kids think they did something wrong when they move to a foster home. But foster homes are for helping kids!* Tell kids why they are in foster care. For example: *You are staying with us* (or *with your foster family*) *because your mom is working out some problems with her social worker.* Children often find their changing emotions confusing too. One minute they may feel happy about their new home, the next minute they may feel worried, sad, or angry. Children may worry that liking foster parents would be disloyal to their birth parents. Healing words may include: *Sometimes you might feel happy you are staying with a foster family, and sometimes you might feel sad. That's okay. When kids live with a foster family, they have lots of different feelings.*

COMMITMENT

Children with so many losses may worry that they will lose you too. Reassure children that you will be there for them through the hard times as well as the happy times. Healing words include: *I will take care of you when you like me, and I will take care of you when you are mad at me. Even when you have really big feelings, I will still be your foster mom* (or *foster dad, teacher, day care mom,* or *social worker*). When it is time for children to move away, help children with a planned goodbye. Celebrating the time you have had together and acknowledging the importance of the child's experience with photographs or a memory book can be helpful.

HOPE

Children need to look to the future with hope. The harder it is today, the more important it is to have hope that tomorrow may be better. Help children express their hopes, dreams, and wishes. Use language that conveys the possibility of change and a better tomorrow. Help children have a wide—rather than a narrow—sense of future. Healing words include: *This was a hard day. Tomorrow will be a new day. We can work together to have a better day tomorrow.*

From Pain to Promise
Improving the lives of young children in foster care

About 150,000 children under age five are placed in foster care each year. Young children receiving protective services are often impacted by poverty, substance abuse, and family violence, as well as child abuse and neglect. Their physical health, emotional health, and development are at risk. They may have problems ranging from lead poisoning, low birth weight, and asthma to language delays and emotional and behavioral problems.

Improving the lives of young children in foster care is an investment in the future. High quality support of at-risk children and their families can increase school success, reduce criminal justice involvement, and support healthy relationships. The economic benefits of investment in early education and support far exceed the costs.

Resources for understanding the challenges of—and planning support for—young children in foster care include:

ChildTrauma Academy

The ChildTrauma Academy is a nonprofit organization whose mission is to help improve the lives of traumatized and maltreated children in three primary ways: education, service delivery, and program consultation. The article "Helping Traumatized Children," as well as other free resources, is available on the academy's Web site, www.childtrauma.org. Free online courses, including "The Cost of Caring: Secondary Traumatic Stress and the Impact of Working with High-Risk Children and Families," are available at www.childtraumaacademy.com.

Cobb, Kathy. "The ABCs of Early Childhood Development." *The Region,* Minneapolis: Federal Reserve Bank of Minneapolis, December 2003.

This article summarizes arguments and commentary made at a fall 2003 conference, "The Economics of Early Childhood Development: Lessons for Economic Policy." Discussion revolves around the question, "Are we investing enough in early childhood development?" It can be accessed at www.minneapolisfed.org.

Dicker, Sheryl, Elysa Gordon, and Jane Knitzer. "Improving the Odds for the Healthy Development of Young Children in Foster Care." National Center for Children in Poverty, Mailman School of Public Health, Columbia University, January, 2002.

This report examines the many challenges young children in foster care face and what child welfare agencies, courts, and other partners can do to improve the physical, developmental, and emotional health of these children. It can be downloaded from the National Center for Children in Povery's Web site: www.nccp.org/publications/pdf/download_114.pdf.

Koplow, Lesley (editor). *Unsmiling Faces: How Preschools Can Heal.* New York: Teachers College Press, 1996.

This book provides early childhood professionals with a framework for understanding the emotional lives of the young children they serve. It combines a theoretical foundation with a practical basis for making preschool classrooms function as therapeutic environments.

The National Foster Parent Association (NFPA)

NFPA is a national organization that strives to support foster parents, and is a consistently strong voice on behalf of all children. Information and many resources, including training and education, are available at NFPA's Web site: www.nfpainc.org.

Prevent Child Abuse America (PCA America)

PCA America works to build awareness, provide education, and inspire hope in everyone involved in the effort to prevent the abuse and neglect of our nation's children. It raises awareness about child abuse through research, initiatives, national publications, and national and local events. Its Web site is www.preventchildabuse.org.

Tobin, L. *What Do You Do with a Child Like This? Inside the Lives of Troubled Children.* Duluth, Minnesota: Whole Person Associates, 1991.

This book offers proven techniques that teachers, parents, counselors, and psychologists can use to cope with behavioral problems and create positive change in children's lives.

About Lifetrack and Families Together

For more than 50 years, Lifetrack has provided services that make a life-changing difference for children and adults with serious challenges to independence and self-sufficiency. Support is provided in the areas of:

- early childhood education and family support

- employment

- rehabilitation therapies

Lifetrack's mission is to build better lives by working together to develop people's strengths. For more information please contact:

Lifetrack
709 University Avenue West
St. Paul, Minnesota 55104-4804
651-227-8471
www.lifetrack-mn.org
mail@lifetrack-mn.org

Families Together is a therapeutic preschool and home visiting program that applies current research on effective early intervention for highly stressed, abused, and neglected children.

About the Author and Illustrator

Julie Nelson holds a B.A. in psychology, is a licensed early childhood teacher, and has graduate certification in Child Abuse Prevention Studies. She has taught in at-risk early childhood settings for most of her 30-year professional career. She is currently the senior teacher at Lifetrack's Families Together program and is on the field faculty for the Center for Early Education and Development at the University of Minnesota. She also provides training in working with highly stressed, hurting, and challenging children, including training presentations at National Association for the Education of Young Children (NAEYC), the Child Welfare League of America conference, Minnesota Association for the Education of Young Children (MnAEYC), Minnesota Children's Mental Health Conference, and Head Start, and in college settings. Julie is passionate about and committed to supporting society's most highly stressed children: those who are in foster care, who are homeless, who have been abused, and/or whose parents are incarcerated or struggle with substance abuse.

Mary Gallagher holds an M.F.A. in studio arts and an M.A.O.T. in occupational therapy. She has been a pediatric occupational therapist for 16 years, working at Lifetrack with Head Start and St. Paul charter schools, and in the clinic. She exhibited her paintings in the Twin Cities and New York City for 10 years after completing her degree at the City University of New York at Brooklyn College in 1989. In recent years, she has focused primarily on creating art installations in public spaces and illustrating books.

Other Great Books from Free Spirit

Families Change
by Julie Nelson,
illustrated by Mary Gallagher
32 pp.; color illustrations; paperback;
9" x 9". For ages 4–10.

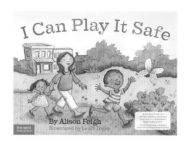

I Can Play It Safe
by Alison Feigh,
illustrated by Laura Logan
32 pp.; color illustrations; hardcover;
10¼" x 7¾". For ages 4–8.

Zach Rules Series
by William Mulcahy,
illustrated by
Darren McKee
32 pp.; color illustrations;
hardcover; 8¼" x 8¼".
For ages 5–8.

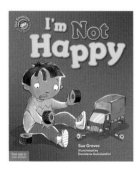   

Our Emotions and Behavior Series
by Sue Graves,
illustrated by
Desideria Guicciardini
28 pp.; color illustrations;
hardcover; 7¾" x 9½".
For ages 4–8.

The Weird Series
by Erin Frankel,
illustrated by Paula Heaphy
48 pp.; color illustrations;
paperback; 9½" x 8".
For ages 5–9.

Interested in purchasing multiple quantities and receiving volume discounts?
Contact edsales@freespirit.com or call 1.800.735.7323 and ask for Education Sales.

Many Free Spirit authors are available for speaking engagements, workshops, and keynotes.
Contact speakers@freespirit.com or call 1.800.735.7323.

For pricing information, to place an order, or to request a free catalog, contact:
Free Spirit Publishing Inc. • **toll-free 800.735.7323** • **help4kids@freespirit.com** • **www.freespirit.com**